Dec. 5004

Nancy,
Thank you for your _____ citizens
who benefit from the Urbana Park District's
programs & services.

Mike

CAROUSEL
OF
CARING

CAROUSEL
OF
CARING

THE CAROUSEL HORSES
OF CHAMPAIGN COUNTY, ILLINOIS
A project to benefit
UNITED WAY OF CHAMPAIGN COUNTY

80 years of caring

www.SportsPublishingLLC.com

ISBN: 1-58261-997-2

Publisher: Peter L. Bannon and Joseph J. Bannon Sr.
Senior managing editor: Susan M. Moyer
Art director: K. Jeffrey Higgerson
Book design: Heidi Norsen
Cover design: Heidi Norsen
Project manager: Heidi Norsen
Imaging: Heidi Norsen
Proofreader: Mark E. Zulauf
Vice president of sales and marketing: Kevin King

Printed in The United States of America

Sports Publishing L.L.C.
804 North Neil Street
Champaign, IL 61820

Phone: 1-877-424-2665
Fax: 217-363-2073
www.SportsPublishingLLC.com

DEDICATION

THIS BOOK IS DEDICATED TO CAROL SCHARLAU

For committing 14 years of service,
devotion, and enthusiasm to
United Way of Champaign County
and the people of our community.

FOREWORD

BY TAMMY LEMKE
United Way President and CEO

and

STEVE TOCK
2004 United Way Board Chair

Since we began as the Champaign-Urbana Community Chest in 1924, renamed United Fund in 1957 and United Way in 1971, the times may have changed, but our purpose remains the same. It is the mission of United Way of Champaign County to strengthen our community through leadership in mobilizing resources to meet the human care needs of Champaign County.

The year 2004 is a very special one for our community. It is the 80th anniversary of United Way of Champaign County. Reflecting on decades of working together to help others, we wanted to celebrate this milestone in a special way that would create community awareness, mobilize resources, and promote new partnerships. The Carousel of Caring is a tangible and highly visible way to share our successes with the Champaign County community–successes thanks to each and every one of you!

It is with great pleasure that we present to you… the Carousel Horses of Champaign County. The time, talent, and thought each artist put into designing his or her masterpiece exemplifies the word "caring," hence the Carousel of Caring. Each carousel horse has a unique story to tell that is captured by the artists in this book–stories as unique as the thousands of people served by your supportive gifts.

As you look through this book and enjoy the magnificent works of art, please remember the sponsors who made this project possible. Their support enabled us to bring the Carousel into our community for each of you to enjoy. We hope you will take the time to appreciate these beautiful creatures and view the talent that abounds in our community. It is sure to delight and amaze you!

Tammy Lemke   Steve Tock

CAROUSEL
OF
CARING

THE CAROUSEL HORSES
OF CHAMPAIGN COUNTY, ILLINOIS
The Story of the Horses

From cows in Chicago to flamingos in Florida, a variety of animals have captivated young and old alike in cities across the country.

These animals are far different than you anticipate–they are adorned with bright paints, colored beads and glass, silk and bells.

The smiles and laughter that carousels inspire is a century-old tradition—a rich history stretching back 1500 years (International Association of Amusement Parks and Attractions). So what better creature than a carousel horse to celebrate our rich history and commemorate our 80th anniversary in Champaign County!

The horses pranced into town last spring and were stabled at secret locations while undergoing transformations, thanks to the most talented artists in our community and the sponsorship of local workplaces.

After countless hours of work to adorn these masterpieces with everything from photos to leather to 24 karat gold, the horses were ready for their final protective coat.

From billboards to Pepsi cans to newspaper stories, the community followed the progress of the carousel horses with the constant reminder "The Horses are Coming."

Following the eagerly anticipated Carousel preview for United Way Donors, artists, and sponsors at Krannert Center for the Performing Arts, the horses were herded to their display locations where they remain until the auction. The Carousel of Caring will strengthen the human service network of Champaign County with auction proceeds benefiting the United Way of Champaign County Endowment Fund.

Now the horses are here and on display for you and your family to enjoy. It is with great pleasure that United Way of Champaign County introduces our beloved carousel horses to our community. A symbol of our 80 years of caring in Champaign County, the horses serve as a reminder of the caring power of our community. We hope you enjoy them.

THE HORSES ARE COMING

United Way
of Champaign County
what matters.™

THE HORSES

PRESENTED IN ALPHABETICAL
ORDER BY ARTIST

Love Spirit Illuminate Ringmaster Sea Dragon Garden Glory Mascot Pretty Horse Innocence Cozy Un Rayo de Luz Advocate Secret Prairie Palomino Mystic in Nature Universal Folio More Gallop Dresden From Around the World Flashback Day into Night Rise and Shine Silver Linings Spirit Love Garden Blooming Filly Rain Garden Illinois the Prairie Little Horse on the Prairie gilded Grace Snowfire Hope Wish Dream peggy gilded Flight of Dreams Little Ride Shadow Red Wild Rides One Unbridled Saw Sparky Shadow One Daisy Secret Garden Sea Horse Jig Unbridled Spectrum Flight

"FLIGHT OF DREAMS"

JODI D'URSO ADAMS, ARTIST

*"Flight of dreams, through its soft hues and design, which connotes whimsy
and grace, the need we all have for things and peace, was conceived from my
daughter's love of the butterfly. The harmony of the pastel tones harkens to
dreams harbored for the soul and summons the child in us all. To keep an
open mind and to be creative in life's journey."*

PERSONALCARE
www.personalcare.org
Providing health plans in Champaign County since 1984.

 CAROUSEL OF CARING

"GALLOP MORE"

SANDRA AHTEN, ARTIST
www.spiritofsandra.com

"I am so inspired by the activists and movers and shakers of our community. I wanted to pay homage to them—to those who go the extra mile—who gallop more.

Gallop More is galloping through a field of poppies. Poppies symbolize pleasure and imagination. I get great pleasure through painting and using my imagination so it seemed like a perfect fit.

In this hectic time in which we live, I think we all gallop more. My hope is that as folks admire Gallop More, they will use their own imagination to find ways to have great pleasure as they gallop more through this world."

THE NEWS-GAZETTE
www.news-gazette.com
Locally owned and operated media company; committed to
providing readers with accurate, timely and useful information.

"FOLIO UNIVERSALE"

STEPHANIE ATKINS, K.C. ELHARD, JACKIE ERDMAN, JENNIFER HAIN, KATHLEEN KERN, OZZIE MEZA, WENDY SHELBURNE, ARTISTS

"Folio Universale runs through the winds of information, picking up books, movies, sound recordings, images, stone and paper, ink and code. She is the spirit of libraries as collections of the human experience and forums for the exchange of ideas.

It is inspiring, as librarians, to work surrounded by a wealth of information. We hope that Folio Universale will instill the same sense of wonder of the diversity that libraries contain and the learning that they support."

UNIVERSITY OF ILLINOIS LIBRARY AT URBANA-CHAMPAIGN
www.library.uiuc.edu
Largest public university library in the world with
collections containing more than 22 million items.

CAROUSEL OF CARING

  CAROUSEL OF CARING

"MYSTIC IN NATURE"

JEANNINE BESTOSO, ARTIST
www.creationartstudios.com

"Mystic is representative of the richness and the healing power of the outdoors. She is a horse on a journey in search of her true self and her original goodness. She feels a calling and a connection to nature and knows it holds the answer to many of life's mysteries. Experiencing connectedness through earth's primordial ground and its nurturing elements she is transformed. She radiates the brilliance of the sun and the light of the stars and the moon. Her spirit and energy are renewed and displayed through the tremendous power of her true colors. Filled with dignity and splendor, flowers, butterflies, and more grace her colorful form. Mystic is synchronizing in mind and body invoking the energy of basic goodness."

CHAMPAIGN SURPLUS STORE
www.champaignsurplus.com
Rugged Outdoor–Since 1947.

"PRAIRIE PALOMINO:
AN ODE TO CHAMPAIGN COUNTY, ILLINOIS"

HARRY BREEN, ARTIST
www.harrybreen.com

"Guiseppe Arcimboldo was a sixteenth century artist who painted at the court of the Hapsbourg emperors. He is best known for his allegorical portraits in which heads are composed of fruit and vegetables among other things. I painted my horse as an allegorical portrait 'a la Arcimboldo.'

For my subject, I chose what has been a dominant theme in my work since I came to Champaign-Urbana forty-six years ago—the prairie landscape of Champaign County. My hope is that the finished horse expresses the goodness, fertility, and visual richness of the prairie land and its spaces."

PRAIRIE GARDENS
Bringing every season, every style
and idea home to you for 40 years.

CAROUSEL OF CARING

  CAROUSEL OF CARING

"GARDEN GLORY"
LISLE C. WISEMAN CASPER, ARTIST

*"I was inspired by the rich Illinois soil and the abundance of beautiful flowers
you see around the area. I selected dark chocolate brown as the base color for
my carousel horse, and then covered it with roses, pansies, and ivy, in celebration
of a Midwestern flower garden. The base, which the horse rests on, is my memory
of riding on a carousel as a small child. The world swirling past as I rode on.
A dark horse, yet full of joy—that is why it is called Garden Glory."*

COZAD ASSET MANAGEMENT, INC.
www.cozadassetmgmt.com
Providing sound financial advice since 1972.

"SEAHORSE"
AFFECTIONATELY KNOWN AS BOB

CHARTER SILLS, ARTISTS
www.chartersills.com

"We wanted our design to make people smile and laugh. Something that would add a little extra happiness into their lives. The world has become much too serious and sometimes a little silliness is needed.

Our seahorse is a world traveler, bringing along all sorts of ocean creatures that he has come across during his travels.

Sometimes laughter truly is the best medicine, and sometimes a (sea)horse is a (sea)horse, of course, of course, especially when the horse is wearing swim fins."

MEYER CAPEL, A PROFESSIONAL CORPORATION
www.meyercapel.com
Focusing their practices on a broad array of legal issues to serve individuals and businesses in the Champaign-Urbana community and across the country.

CAROUSEL OF CARING

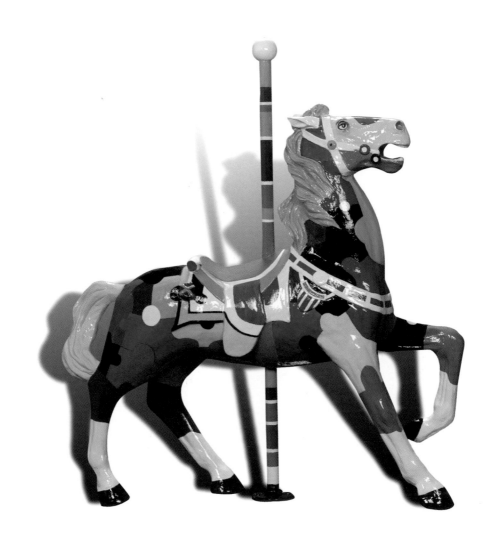

  CAROUSEL OF CARING

"JIG SAW"

ALYCE CHESKA AND JAMES H. LYNCH, ARTISTS

"Jig Saw represents the joining together of different shapes, sizes and colors into a unified image echoing United Way's mandate for bringing together varied elements to create a caring community."

CLARK-LINDSEY VILLAGE
www.clark-lindsey.com
Premier senior living community centered on quality living.

"UNBRIDLED SPECTRUM"

MARY ANN DIXON, MIKE FELDMAN,
JULIE KUKREJA, JOANNE LEE, ARTISTS

*"Unbridled Spectrum pulls together both the creative/artistic community
and the business/technology community in service of the philanthropic
community. The horse itself is naturalistic, while the tackle shows a blend
of motifs from both technology and decorative arts. The word spectrum
means not just the narrow band of visible light, but all the bands which
technology lets us use to communicate; communication which is truly
unbridled when we use all the tools that art and technology provide."*

MOTOROLA URBANA-CHAMPAIGN DESIGN CENTER
www.urbana-motorola.com
Focusing on the development and testing of software which
becomes part of the state-of-the-art Motorola cellular phones.

  CAROUSEL OF CARING

"PEGGY"

CHRIS EVANS, ARTIST

"As I began working on my carousel horse, I thought of the current interest in the Olympics being held again as it was so many years ago in Athens, Greece. According to legend the logo of my employer was a winged Mercury. How fitting to use this symbol for my carousel horse, affectionately called Peggy."

NEWSTALK 1400 WDWS–LITE ROCK 97.5 WHMS
www.wdws.com
Newstalk 1400 WDWS news, information, and sports for East Central Illinois.
Lite Rock 97.5 WHMS Champaign-Urbana's official at-work station.

"GILDED GRACE"

VICTOR FEIN AND SOOZIE ROBINSON, ARTISTS

www.a-zoomart.com

"It is through the heart and hands of prosperity that we are fortunate enough to give. Everyone who has been a part of the making of Grace felt the force of giving.

"Even more beautiful than the horse itself is the act of humanity that revolves around her. All the gold and scrolls and ornate leather and beads cannot compare to the grace in which we give. Her strength and beauty come from the will of the human spirit to do good and to give back as best they can to others in need. And so she comes to you in all her glory not just a decorated horse but a gilded grace."

COMMUNITY FOUNDATION OF EAST CENTRAL ILLINOIS

www.cfeci.org

Serving as a major catalyst for philanthropic assistance to the residents of East Central Illinois since 1972.

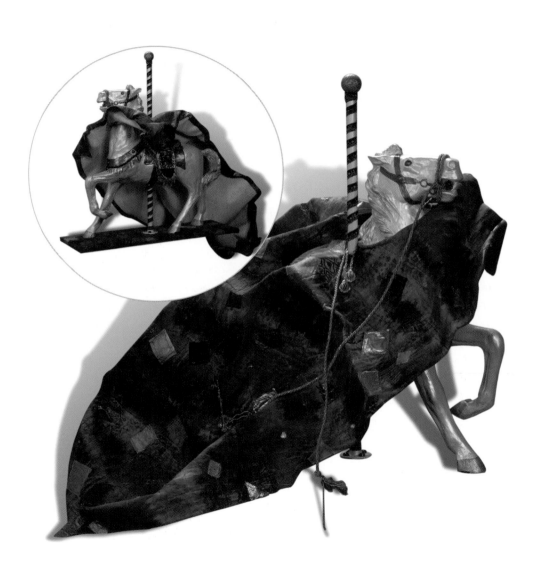

CAROUSEL OF CARING

"SNOWFIRE"

DEBORAH FELL, ARTIST
www.deborahfell.com

"I always loved horses and as a little girl I saw the movie Snowfire. *It was about a beautiful white horse that was kind, smart and helpful to all of the other horses. A favorite game as a child was playing horses. I always got to be the head of the herd because I could run the fastest. When I was eight my mother left and I did not see her for many years. Around my 10th birthday, my mother sent me a note asking what I wanted for my gift. I sent her a note back asking her to nickname me Snowfire. Somewhere I still have the card from my mother which read… for your birthday, I nickname you Snowfire.*

So here she is—Snowfire at fifty! But now Snowfire has an art quilt cape, meant to be a tangible reminder to never lose hope in our lives, no matter what the circumstances."

CARLE FOUNDATION HOSPITAL AND
CARLE CLINIC ASSOCIATION
www.carle.com
Working to provide a comprehensive spectrum of
health care to the residents of East Central Illinois.

"HOPE WISH DREAM"

JOSEPH W. GALLO, ARTIST

"The creative intent of this horse is to honor the countless wishes and hopes of so many children who have been helped by United Way. Eighty stars for celebrating 80 years of tireless service for so many in need. I can only hope that the simple and childlike quality of this Matisse-influenced carousel horse drives home the idea that on any given star-filled night, children anywhere in need are wishing, hoping and dreaming of a better life."

BANKCHAMPAIGN, N.A.
www.bankchampaign.com
Committed to expanding the financial horizons of our customers.

CAROUSEL OF CARING

 CAROUSEL OF CARING

"RISE & SHINE"

PATRICK HARNESS, ARTIST
www.patrickharness.com

"Rise & Shine represents a hot summer's morning in Central Illinois.
The corn and beans are thriving in spite of our volatile weather.
The heat of the day stretches before us, and the promise
of a bumper crop hangs in the air."

FRAMER'S MARKET
www.framersmarket.net
Custom Picture Framing & Gallery Since 1981.

"DAY INTO NIGHT"

MICHELLE HARRINGTON (HAUG), ARTIST

"Having a family, I'm well aware of the potential of our children's hopes, wishes and dreams. The vast decisions and opportunities we are faced with everyday reminds me that life is ever changing and filled with endless possibilities.

"Day into Night represents the opposites that occur throughout our lives. With each new day rises a new hope of possibilities and opportunity. With each night we are able to dream of a fresh start of a new day."

CHRISTIE CLINIC
www.christieclinic.com
Medicine for Your Life–Celebrating 75 Years

CAROUSEL OF CARING

"FLASHBACK"

BRYAN HEATON, ARTIST

"For the 80th anniversary of United Way of Champaign County, I wanted to create a work that would remind viewers of the many people United Way has helped in the past. I wanted to remind people that the community we live in today is built on the spirit of our past, a past that United Way has helped to make strong. A past that now strides forward into the future where the spirit and generosity of those who came before will help support and keep safe those who need help now. Flashback is a reminder of good things from the past, but his spirit is ever striding forward."

CHAMPAIGN COUNTY CHAMBER OF COMMERCE AND
CHAMPAIGN COUNTY ECONOMIC DEVELOPMENT CORPORATION
www.champaigncounty.org
www.champaigncountyedc.org
Working together to promote economic development
and prosperity in Champaign County.

"FROM AROUND THE WORLD"

ERICA J. HENRY, ARTIST

"I painted my horse as a representation of how people from around the world come to our community in search of learning. Our community is made up of all types of people, cultures, and ethnic groups that have moved here to better their lives in some way. I feel that I can represent, on a small scale, some of the places from around the world and connect them to our wonderful, diverse and genuinely unique community. From Around the World truly does show that the population of Champaign County is made up of people who really are from around the world."

PARKLAND COLLEGE FOUNDATION
www.parkland.edu
Creating brighter futures.

CAROUSEL OF CARING

"SPARKY"

DIANE LADUKE, ARTIST

*"In creating Sparky, the process I was hoping to achieve was reflective
movement and synchronicity of elements. Sparky was created with
the use of mirrors, glitter, and multi-layered paint. I believe all works of
art reflect their surroundings; Sparky will always be a work in progress
as he mirrors his environment and ever-changing landscape."*

HEALTH ALLIANCE MEDICAL PLANS
www.healthalliance.org
Leading provider-sponsored health insurer in the Midwest.

"SHADOW"

JAN McCRACKEN, ARTIST

"Shadow is a horse with a very active imagination.

"He sees shapes both familiar and fantastic everywhere:
up in the clouds in the sky, in silhouettes cast by the low evening
sun, and even in the pattern of his own coat.

"Shadow celebrates the ability that exists in everyone to look beyond
reality and see the possibilities that exist within our imagination."

UNIVERSITY OF ILLINOIS EMPLOYEES CREDIT UNION
www.uiecu.org
Serving the U of I community since 1932.

  CAROUSEL OF CARING

"ONE WILD RIDE"
NILSA ALMENAS MUNIZ AND BRIAN J. SULLIVAN, ARTISTS
www.briansullivanart.com

*"Like the electrons in motion around an atom, our community is made up
of many diverse and dynamic elements that are unique and special to our community.
One Wild Ride symbolizes United Way's focus on helping people whose lives have
been disturbed by some event or crisis. It's about people and caring.
It's about community and helping the people who make up our community."*

KRAFT FOODS–CHAMPAIGN
www.kraft.com
One of the world's largest manufacturing facilities,
producing many of America's favorite KRAFT brands.

"SHADOW RED"

HUA NIAN, ARTIST
www.huanian.com

"Shadow Red is a spirit emerging from the dark, carrying messages from the deep past. From its intense red, shadowed by dark colors but burning through the body, I was trying to invoke the energy of a force... a force of curiosity, mysterious and stubborn, about who we are and where we are. This force has never diminished, but has only grown stronger with new discoveries and inventions. In our modern age, I find myself always returning for inspiration to myths and the primitive. The strong contrasts—black and white, warm and cool, painterly and decorative—express feelings of playfulness and magic; the pole is a shaman's staff of incantation."

COLWELL
A PATTERSON COMPANY
www.colwellsystems.com
Provider of healthcare forms and supplies.

  CAROUSEL OF CARING

"LITTLE HORSE ON THE PRAIRIE"

LONNA PRUITT, ARTIST

"The prairie-scape of Champaign County has changed over the last 80 years, but through it all, United Way has grown and stayed strong. With the help of the organization, our prairie has changed into a place where thoughts are collaborated, architecture is showcased, and the arts are celebrated. With this in mind, I could not have thought of a better way to acknowledge United Way of Champaign County's 80th anniversary than to showcase the county that it serves through a pictorial celebration of the Central Illinois prairie."

"ILLINOIS"

TONI PUTNAM, ARTIST

"This is a very different landscape from where I grew up in the Northeast with its hills and valleys, but I have grown to love this change, this flatness, in all its seasons. There are the skies with every possible version of the clouds, storms that can be watched approaching and leaving, strange mists rising in the early morning from plowed fields or small ponds. There are endless fields stretching to infinity and wonderful rows of trees bent by the wind. So I am constantly taking pictures and sketching these things that catch my eye."

URBANA PARK DISTRICT
www.urbanaparks.org
Offering 22 parks and hundreds of recreation programs to
area residents that enrich and improve quality of life.

  CAROUSEL OF CARING

"RAIN GARDEN"

REBECCA RENWICK, ARTIST

"I chose to create a mosaic horse covered entirely with Venetian glass. These glass tiles are the same composition as those made thousands of years ago and have a very unique quality to them. The transparency and luminosity reminded me of water and its reflective nature. I felt this application was most appropriate based on the fluid nature of Hydroponics."

HICKORY POINT BANK & TRUST
www.hickorypointbank.com
Committed to providing exceptional service in a
warm professional banking environment.

"BLOOMING FILLY"

CHRIS ROGERS, ARTIST

"Who can experience a carousel without envisioning the atmosphere of an old-fashioned amusement park of lush green grass and blooming spring flowers circling a pack of graceful animals bobbing up and down to the organ music, lead by a beautiful white filly. Blooming Filly captures the excitement of the viewer being there once again, as she moves magically to her music, her golden mane flowing in the breeze, and her exquisitely colorful floral body exclaiming the aura of the traditional carousel."

ALFORD GROUP EXECUTIVE SEARCH
www.ag-es.com
Helping not-for-profit organizations
strengthen through staffing solutions.

50

  CAROUSEL OF CARING

"SILVER LININGS"

TAYA ROSS, ARTIST

"Silver Linings captures the essence of what United Way does for people in our community. United Way provides a support in difficult times... help in finding the silver lining inside the dark cloud. It is a belief in the potential for transformation."

WCIA 3-YOUR NEWS LEADER
www.wcia.com
Serving Champaign-Urbana for over 50 years.

"LOVE"

LEI SHANBHAG, ARTIST
www.leishanbhag.com

"Love is a label for the force that sustains this Universe. It is more than a universal language. Love binds the animate and the inanimate in an unending dance of existence. Yet the human expression of love takes a diversity of forms: intentions, desires, actions, words, symbols, gestures, sounds, and others. In its basest form, love leads to physical attraction. At its finest, love leads to the realization of one's primordial relationship to the divine. This work reminds us that love manifests itself in every culture and language, and is a universal bond tying us together."

UPCLOSE MARKETING & PRINTING
www.upcloseprinting.com
Creating and developing innovative ideas to accomplish
the best solutions for your business goals.

  CAROUSEL OF CARING

"SPIRIT"

JENNY SOUTHLYNN, ARTIST

"I had recently suffered the loss of my mother but had not actually grieved. It wasn't until I was riding through a field in Mahomet one winter evening on my friend Annette's horse, Aquilia, when I felt Aquilia's silent acceptance of my pain and loss. For the first time, the tears fell and I let them flow. It was her spirit I sensed. No words, just the warmth of her body. It freed me and we rode like we had wings. It was a blessing, one I'll never forget. My hope is that everyone finds that sense of acceptance and experiences the flight of their spirit on a winged horse."

"ILLUMINATE"

ROBB SPRINGFIELD, ARTIST

"The design of Illuminate reflects what United Way means to so many families and individuals in the community. The light and hope that can be diminished by life's day-to-day pressures can be uplifted by the programs and determined focus of United Way, the magic of riding a carousel, the brass ring and a child's wish… anything is possible and just at the end of your fingertips. The seat of the carousel horse transports you and is a thing of beauty and represents United Way. Illuminate creates a 'Wizard of Oz' type feel, moving you from the black and white world of daily existence to the colorful childlike dream of possibilities."

UNIVERSITY OF ILLINOIS AT URBANA-CHAMPAIGN
www.uiuc.edu
One of the world's leading public universities looked to internationally for
leadership in research, education, and engagement with critical societal issues.

  CAROUSEL OF CARING

"RINGMASTER"

GREGORY STALLMEYER, ARTIST
www.gscustoms.com

"The happiest rider on the carousel of life is the one who is constantly reaching for the brass ring. We are the ringmasters of our lives and by attempting to be the best, living our days to the fullest, and most of all giving to others; we can realize our true potential.

"The bright colors and bold shapes in the design of this horse echo this sentiment and represent the vibrancy with which we should all strive to live."

STRATEGIC MARKETING & MAILING
www.strategicmail.com
Exceeding your expectations.

"SEA DRAGON"

MORAKOT VANNAVAT, ARTIST

"The design of this horse is the artist's depiction borrowed from a children's fable from Thailand. The story is of a father and daughter who are on a journey through a wonderland filled with blue skies, lush forests, and deep blue oceans. The daughter, who is pregnant while riding the Sea Dragon, is protected by its magical powers throughout her journeys with her father. As the story goes, the daughter gives birth to a son who in turn rides the Sea Dragon with his grandfather at his side. The grandson then uses the magic of the Sea Dragon to conquer evil throughout the wonderland in which he, his mother, and his grandfather live."

PEPSI-COLA CHAMPAIGN-URBANA BOTTLING CO.
www.pepsiworld.com
Family Owned and Operated Since 1953.

  CAROUSEL OF CARING

"DRESDEN"

BETH KIDD WIESE, ARTIST

"Once upon a time, there were princes and kings,
Who commissioned artists to create beautiful things
There were sculptors, painters and composers anew.
These artists changed the way we see
And to this day, teach us the importance of creativity.

"Dresden the carousel horse was created in part;
To bring to his audience this same gift of art.
With inspiration from the baroque ornate,
The idea of a sleigh horse soon took shape.
Dresden arose from one sculptor's mind,
His tapestries and tassels, the artist divined.
Her vision of Dresden evolved and took form
Her friends and supporters watched a plain horse transform.
The horse is now completed and ready to share
It is sent forth with fondness, excitement and a well wisher's prayer."

SCHNUCKS
www.schnucks.com
The friendliest store in town.

"MASCOT"
ALYCE CHESKA AND JAMES H. LYNCH, ARTISTS
United Way of Champaign County, Sponsor

"INNOCENCE"

HEATHER LEE FOX, ARTIST
Champaign County CASA, Sponsor

"COZY"

MICHELE M. HILLARD, ARTIST
Crisis Nursery, Sponsor

CAROUSEL OF CARING

"PRETTY HORSE"

PAIGE, COLLEEN AND WILL WITH DEENA LOVE, ARTISTS
Developmental Services Center, Sponsor

"UN RAYO DE LUZ"

AMY MARTINEZ, ARTIST
Catholic Charities, Sponsor

CAROUSEL OF CARING

"ADVOCATE"

ROBERTA R. MORRIS, ARTIST
A Woman's Fund, Sponsor

"SECRET GARDEN"

JESSICA SAPP, ARTIST
Planned Parenthood of East Central Illinois, Sponsor

CAROUSEL OF CARING

"DAISY"

KEM WIGGINS, ARTIST
Girl Scouts–Green Meadows Council, Sponsor

UNITED WAY
OF CHAMPAIGN
COUNTY
HISTORY

COMMUNITY CHEST   (1924–1957)
UNITED FUND   (1957–1971)
UNITED WAY   (1971–Present)

1924–Champaign and Urbana Chambers of Commerce organized Champaign-Urbana Community Chest. The first year's campaign raised $42,667 for nine member agencies: Anti-Tuberculosis League, Boy Scouts, Family Welfare Society, Girl Scouts, Red Cross, Salvation Army, University YMCA, Urbana Railroad YMCA, and Humane Society.

1933–The Council of Social Services was created to provide year-round planning and coordination of community health and welfare services.

1945–Champaign-Urbana Community Chest expanded to include all of Champaign County, becoming Champaign County Community Chest.

1957–Community Chest became the United Fund of Champaign County, Inc.

1957–"Give Where You Work" eliminated door-to-door solicitation and introduced company match for work and payroll deduction.

1961–"Fair Share" plan unveiled with the first-year goal of $8.00 per employee.

1971–United Fund became United Way of Champaign County.

1978–The fund distribution process was recognized with the formation of five allocation panels of volunteers: Health, Youth, Family, Community, and New Services.

1981–The Voluntary Action Center joined forces with United Way and became the Volunteer Center of Champaign County.

1985–The leadership giving program, Pillars, was established. The program grew from 131 Pillars in 1985 to 1,312 today.

1991–16 AFL-CIO members graduated in the first United Way–AFL-CIO Union Counselor Training Program.

1995–United Way announced its first Alexis de Tocqueville members.

1998–The Presidents' Council was established.

2002–United Way and the University of Illinois partnered to sponsor the Success By 6® Initiative.

2004–United Way celebrates 80 years of caring in Champaign County.

REFLECTIONS
THROUGH
THE
DECADES

COMMUNITY CHEST   (1924–1957)
UNITED FUND   (1957–1971)
UNITED WAY   (1971–Present)

STU MAMER
1955 Campaign Chair
1957 Board President

JERRY O'NEIL
1968 Campaign Chair

1950s–The goal of the Community Chest drive I headed in 1955 was less than one-tenth of this year's goal. The merger of Community Chest with the United Health Fund in 1957 created the United Fund, now United Way, of which I was the first president. The growth since then has provided much greater care for more individuals who are most in need.

1960s–United Way was based on a sound concept that stands the test of time. Develop an organization to concentrate fundraising for several charities. This allows the charitable organization to perform their respective duties without major fundraising responsibilities. The community wins as they have only one solicitation instead of more than a score. It's a WIN-WIN.

LOTT THOMAS
1977 Board President

GEORGE SODEMANN
1985 Campaign Chair
1987 Board President
1995 Pillar Chair
1997-98 United Way of
Illinois Board Chair

1980s–One of the highlights of the '80s was the creation of our nationally recognized leadership giving program, Pillars. We reintroduced countywide community kick-off events to increase public awareness and expanded efforts to assess community needs and be more accountable to donors. This was also a period of transition into a more business, corporate structure. Incidentally, we also jumped into the technology age with our first computer, a seven-inch screen Apple.

1970s–In 1938, when my father was President of the Community Chest, the predecessor to United Way, there was a much greater sense of "community" than we had in the 1970s and certainly than we have today. As government programs increased in the 1970s, particularly in the human services area, United Way served an increasingly important role in raising awareness of unmet community needs.

ZELEMA HARRIS
1994 Campaign Chair

MARY McGRATH
2003 Board Chair

1990s–Every citizen who is able to give should see first hand the lives touched by United Way of Champaign County. I vividly recall the year that I served as Campaign Chair. During that year I visited thirteen of the United Way partner agencies. Crisis Nursery, Center for Women in Transition and A Woman's Fund were three of the agencies that I visited. The women and children being served by these agencies still hold a special place in my heart. I often wonder what would happen to the women and children served by these and other United Way agencies if it were not for a community of givers. We care about those who need support and protection. I am grateful to live in a community where giving to others is one of our core values.

2000s–During my association with United Way of Champaign County, the organization has evolved from a fundraiser for agencies to a fundraiser whose primary purpose is to fill the needs of the people of Champaign County. Programs are identified that have the most impact and that serve a need. Financial resources are then provided. United Way takes its role seriously, and the result is a much better community for everyone.

INDEX

CAROUSEL OF CARING

WE SINCERELY THANK THE FOLLOWING BUSINESSES AND INDIVIDUALS WHO,
IN ADDITION TO OUR WONDERFUL ARTISTS AND SPONSORS, HELPED MAKE
THE CAROUSEL OF CARING SUCH A GREAT SUCCESS!

40 North 88 West

Adams Outdoor Advertising

Art Mart

Awards Ltd.

Vanda Bidwell

Bill Bland/Action Auction

Blue Star Collision Center

Busey Bank

Tom Cain/ReMax

Carter's Furniture

Champaign County Courthouse

Pat Chapel

Colwell Systems

Cowpainters

The Great Impasta

Darrell Hoemann

Kennedy's at Stone Creek

Krannert Center for the Performing Arts

Marketplace Mall

CAROUSEL OF CARING

Milo's Restaurant

Naperville United Way

The News-Gazette

Robert K. O'Daniell

One Main Development

Pages for All Ages

Pepsi-Cola Champaign Urbana Bottling Co.

Prairie Gardens

Premium Brands

Schnucks

Robin Scholz

Silvercreek

Sports Publishing L.L.C.

Sun Singer Wine & Spirits

WCIA 3–Your News Leader

University of Illinois Willard Airport

UpClose Marketing and Printing

We also appreciate the support of

one anonymous sponsor.